The Song of Love

By Joan Walsh Anglund

The Song of Love

by

Joan Walsh Anglund

Charles Scribner's Sons / New York

CHARLES SCRIBNER'S SONS
Macmillan Publishing Company
866 Third Avenue, New York, NY 10022
Collier Macmillan Canada, Inc.

Library of Congress Cataloging-in-Publication Data

Anglund, Joan Walsh.
    The song of love.

    I. Title.
PS3551.N47S6   1987   811'.54   86-29818
ISBN 0-684-18767-1

Composition by Heritage Printers, Inc., Charlotte, North Carolina
Manufactured by Fairfield Graphics, Fairfield, Pennsylvania

First Edition

Macmillan books are available at special discounts for bulk purchases
for sales promotions, premiums, fund-raising, or educational use.
For details, contact:

                    Special Sales Director
                    Macmillan Publishing Company
                    866 Third Avenue
                    New York NY 10022

10 9 8 7 6 5 4 3

Printed in the United States of America

For my dear friend Maggie Meredith,

with love

Nature

    instructs

    with unvarying grace,

        through every season

            her beauty shimmers,

        teaching us

            the unity

                of Life.

We are given

       Beauty

   that we may learn its ways.

We are given

       Hope

   that we may begin our Journey.

We are given

       Friends

   that we may see God's love

       shining through to us

            from their eyes.

The Song of Love

    never stills

  . . . though the lark is gone,

    its melody

       remains.

We fly toward Forever

on

unknowing wings

Our destination

hidden

in the mists.

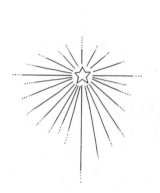

The night is dark

        that has no Star

   . . . how dark the heart

        when Love is far.

The wise man

    concerns himself

    not

    with the chatter

        of today and yesterday

. . . but listens instead

    for the Voice

        of Eternity.

Sometimes

a Joy

may be born

out of much pain

. . . as a Rose

may blossom

amidst

many thorns.

My own thought

establishes

the boundaries

of my possibilities.

Go to the mountains

     . . . and listen to the hills,

   for in their great silence

     they speak the Truth more clearly

  than

   all

    the voices of the city.

He who would lead

        must first follow.

He who would hear

        must first listen.

He who would receive the spirit

        must first

                be emptied of the self.

Release

the Past.

Receive

the Now.

To the extent

        that

    you want something

           from someone . . .

    to that exact degree

        can you be hurt.

For it is desire

        that brings us pain

   . . . as it is Love

        that brings us

           Joy!

As a light

      through the darkness,

As a lifeline

      through the tides,

As a saving hope

      in times of deep despair

      . . . is my *Friend!*

The mind

        that dreams

    can also

        destroy

   . . . such Power

        has a thought!

Happiness

            is a choice,

     not

       an accident.

Ecstasy

         is given,

              but Happiness

                 is our own

                    creation.

It matters little

      whether J am loved or not.

    It matters greatly

      that J love.

That which you hold

   . . . you shall lose.

That which you set free

   . . . is yours

          forever.

The truest slavery

      is Avarice

  . . . no chain can bind us

         as completely

            as our *own* Ambition.

Unless
     we are made new again
     . . . we cannot see
       . . . we cannot hear.

All words
     are old words.

All experience
     is old experience

     . . . the only Truth
          is NOW
     . . . in *this* instant!

The Heart
     that awakens
       lives
         and changes.

The Heart
     that sleeps
     . . . comes
        again and again
     to learn the lesson
      it has refused
         for so long
           to see.

Fear

      in my throat

    . . . and blessings,

         just beyond my reach!

If I am filled
            with Envy
    . . . I cannot be filled
                with Abundance.

If I am filled
            with Desire
    . . . I cannot be filled
                with Peace.

If I am filled
            with Fear
    . . . I cannot be filled
                with Love.

How often we reach
                for that
                    which could never
                            be ours,
        and discard
                the jewel
                that was to bring
                    our greatest
                            joy!

That which must Ask

 . . . cannot know.

That which knows

 . . . has no need

 of Question.

Love has no age
        . . . or color,
    knows no boundary
        . . . or border,

    but is a Gift
        . . . bestowed equally
        upon *all*
        who will receive it.

The body tires
              . . . but the spirit continues.

Stay not
          so concerned

      with the body

              that shall be discarded

. . . no more than,
                  disrobing,

      you would hover

              over the costume
                          worn
                              but

              for an hour.

Oh, *Love*
    that does not doubt,
  Love
    that does not ask,
  Love
    that does not change,
  Love
    that does not falter,

Love
        . . . that comforts
                and protects,
    Love
    that takes not . . .
                but gives all,
      Love
        that says no word
                of Self
        but speaks instead
            with kindest action
                and concern
                    for its
                        Beloved.

How quickly

    Doubt

        can tear the Beauty

    Love

        took so long

            to weave.

And,

    in the end,

   let us hurry Home

     . . . like children

         who, after long play,

    rush happily

       to Loving Arms

     and

      welcome

        Sleep.

The rose shall fade

    . . . the mighty oak

                shall fall

and
    the mountain
               shall crumble
                        into dust.

Love
    alone
        never ends.

JOAN WALSH ANGLUND, the much-loved author-artist of such celebrated titles as *A Friend Is Someone Who Likes You* and *Love Is a Special Way of Feeling*, lives with her family in an eighteenth-century house in Connecticut. Her books, whose sales number in the millions, have been published in England, Germany, Sweden, Denmark, Norway, Spain, Brazil, and South Africa.